Michael S. Woods, M.D.

The World Is A Small Place.

AND THE SMALLER IT GETS, THE MORE IMPORTANT
IT BECOMES THAT WE UNDERSTAND EACH OTHER.

As health care professionals in the United States, we're
likely to count among our patients people from all over the
globe. Hmong in Minneapolis. Chinese in Atlanta. Vietnamese in Wichita. Russians in Denver. Africans in Seattle.
All of the above and more in New York, Chicago, and Los
Angeles.

These various peoples carry with them cultures and
customs that affect the way they interpret the world,
their experiences, and their relationships.

When it comes to health care, the U.S. might have great
technology and dedicated, intelligent health care staff, but
these advantages are lost if our patients can't understand
the "why" and "what" of their care.

If a patient, because of a cultural "disconnect," can't
appreciate what we're prescribing or why it's necessary,
or if the information is delivered in a way that inadvertently
frightens or offends the patient, *how can we fulfill
our mission as health care providers?*

?

THE ANSWER IS PATIENT-CENTERED HEALTH CARE

Take a minute to think of the patient as a customer —how would that change our behavior? We'd be obliged to give the patient what he or she wants. Doing that (within the boundaries of the right medical solution, of course) means being sensitive to each patient's culture-driven expectations.

If patients feel we understand and respect them as individuals, they'll be more likely to trust us and comply with our prescribed therapies and treatments. The greater the trust, the better the outcomes. The better the outcomes, the lower the risk of medical malpractice liability.

Joint Commission Resources has published this guide as a service to our colleagues in the health care industry. The information in this CULTURAL SENSITIVITY POCKET GUIDE comes from www.ggalanti.com and from "Caring for Patients from Different Cultures" by Geri-Ann Galanti, Ph.D. Each section addresses a few core cultural patterns that can lead to misunderstandings. By using this guide, physicians, nurses, and other health care professionals can take an important step toward better patient relationships.

Michael S. Woods, M.D

A WORD OF CAUTION

GENERALIZATIONS SHOULD NOT BE MISTAKEN FOR STEREOTYPES

If I meet Rosa, a Mexican woman, and say to myself, "Rosa is Mexican; she must have a large family," I am stereotyping her. But if I think Mexicans often have large families and then ask Rosa how many people are in her family, I am making a generalization.

A STEREOTYPE is an ending point. No attempt is made to learn whether the individual in question fits the statement. Stereotyping patients can have negative results.

A GENERALIZATION is a beginning point. It indicates common trends, but further information is needed to ascertain whether the statement is appropriate to a particular individual. Generalizations may be inaccurate when applied to specific individuals, but when applied broadly, can indicate common behaviors and shared beliefs. (Of course, there are always differences among individuals.)

A FEW FUNDAMENTALS

Let's look at some core causes for cultural "disconnects" between health care providers and patients, beginning with **VALUES.** Simply put: different cultures promote different values.

Right now, the U.S. culture values such things as money, freedom, independence, privacy, health and fitness, and physical appearance. But another culture—say, the Mbuti of Africa—might value social support. To punish a wrongdoer, the U.S. takes away his money (through a fine of some sort) or his freedom (with incarceration); the Mbuti, on the other hand, punish people by ignoring them When the U.S. health care system makes decisions based on finances, people from a social-centric culture like the Mbuti may not "get it."

Similarly, in the U.S. the value of **INDEPENDENCE** is evident in children moving away from home as soon as financially possible. In other cultures, children might not move out until marriage and often not even then. Our health care providers might tell a patient to "take care of yourself" without considering the role of family members in the dynamics of the individual's daily activities of life.

PRIVACY is also important in the U.S., so hospitals try to limit visiting hours and rarely offer sleeping accommodations for visitors. Many non-Anglo patients, however, would prefer just the opposite. Similarly, the U.S. health care culture values *self-control*, but many patients come from cultures in which *emotional expressiveness* is the norm.

A FEW FUNDAMENTALS

Obviously, similar illustrations could be made for all the things people value. But the point has been made: Understanding people's values is the key to understanding their behavior, for our behavior generally reflects our values.

Another Source of Confusion:

SOCIAL STRUCTURE The U.S. model is egalitarian: in theory, everyone is equal. Status and power come from an individual's achievements rather than from age, sex, family, or occupation. Other cultures, such as Asian, are hierarchical: everyone is not equal. Status comes from age, sex, and occupation. And these differences are considered important.

One way to discuss the impact of culture on our thinking and behavior is through two anthropological concepts:

ETHNOCENTRISM (the view that one's own culture's way of doing things is the right and natural way to do them). Most humans are ethnocentric; that's only natural. But ethnocentrism can impede cross-cultural communication and understanding.

CULTURAL RELATIVISM (the attitude that other ways of doing things are different but equally valid). This is the attitude we should all strive for; it will lead to better communication and trust.

The practitioners of Western health care tend to believe that their approaches to healing are superior to all others. **But the goal of all healing is the same: to help people get well. If different cultures studied each other's techniques with an open mind, the cause of modern medicine would be greatly advanced.**

The best way to begin to appreciate a patient's point of view is to ask a few important questions. And then, listen—*really listen*—to the answers.

We suggest these questions, as suggested by psychiatrist and anthropologist Arthur Kleinman, as a way to establish a meaningful dialogue: [1]

1) What do you think has caused your problem?

2) Why do you think it started when it did?

3) What do you think your sickness does to you? How does it work?

4) How severe is your sickness? Will it have a short or long course?

5) What kind of treatment do you think you should receive?

6) What are the most important results you hope to receive from this treatment?

7) What are the chief problems your sickness has caused for you?

8) What do you fear most about your sickness?

[1] Kleinman, A., L. Eisenberg, and B. Good. (1978) Culture, illness, and care: Clinical lessons from anthropologic and cross-cultural research. *Annals of Internal Medicine* 88: 251-58.

A MNEMONIC FOR HEALTH CARE PROFESSIONALS

One way to remember what questions to ask is to use the following mnemonic:

1. **C**all: What do you call your problem? (This is one way of asking "What do you think is wrong?" It's getting at the patient's perception of the problem. You shouldn't literally ask, "What do you call your problem?" Use "call" to help you remember to ask what *the patient* thinks is wrong.)

The same symptoms may have very different meanings in different cultures and may result in barriers to compliance. For example, among the Hmong, epilepsy is referred to as "the spirit catches you, and you fall down." Seeing epilepsy as spirit possession (which has some positive connotations for the possessed) is very different from seeing it as a disruption of the electrical signals in the brain. This should lead to a very different doctor-patient conversation and might help explain why such a patient may be less anxious than the physician to stop the seizures. Understanding the patient's point of view can help the health care provider deal with potential barriers to compliance.

2. **C**ause: What do you think caused your problem? (This gets at the patient's beliefs regarding the source of the problem.)

Not everyone believes that disease is caused by germs. In some cultures, it is thought to be caused by upset in body balance, breach of taboo (similar to what is seen in the U.S. as diseases due to "sin" and punished by God), or spirit possession. Treatment must be appropriate to the cause, or people will not perceive themselves as cured. Doctors thus need to find out what the patient believes caused the problem and treat that as well. For example, it may sometimes be appropriate to bring in clergy to pray with a patient if the patient believes God is punishing him or her for some transgression.

3. Cope: How do you cope with your condition? (This can also be asked in terms of "What have you done to try to make it better? Who else have you been to for treatment?")

This will provide the health care provider with important information on the use of alternative healers and treatments. Most people will try home remedies before coming to the physician; however, few will share such information due to fear of ridicule or chastisement. It's important that health care providers learn to ask – in a non-judgmental way – because the occasional traditional remedy may be dangerous or could lead to a drug interaction with prescribed medications. This question can also help you discover if a patient has been unable to cope with whatever is going on.

4. Concerns: What are your concerns regarding the condition? (This is really asking, "How does it interfere with your life or your ability to function?") What are your concerns about the recommended treatment?

You want to understand their perception of the course of the illness and the fears they may have about it so you can address their concerns and correct any misconceptions. You also want to know what aspects of the condition pose a problem for the patient; this may help you uncover something very different from what you might have expected. You also want to know a patient's concerns about any treatment you may prescribe. This can help avoid problems of non-adherence, because some patients may have misplaced concerns based upon experience. For example, some patients may not take insulin because they believe insulin causes blindness. They've seen friends and family members go blind after going on insulin, and they incorrectly perceive that as the cause; it's a logical assumption based on observed cause and effect. Unless a health care provider asks, however, you may not elicit such beliefs from the patient, who will simply not take insulin. By asking, the health care provider can correct any misconceptions that can interfere with treatment.

Developed by Stuart Slavin, M.D., Geri-Ann Galanti, Ph.D., and Alice Kuo, M.D.

CAUTION: These are broad generalizations and should not be used to stereotype any individuals.

VALUES, WORLD VIEW, AND COMMUNICATION

- **African American patients, especially older ones, may not trust hospitals.** This is due to studies showing racial disparities in health care, and due to the notorious Tuskegee experiment conducted by the U.S. Public Health Service. African American males with syphilis were left untreated to observe the course of the disease. Results were observed on autopsy. The men who "participated" in the "experiment" were never informed; they were merely told they had "bad blood."

- **African Americans may also be very sensitive to discrimination, even when it is not intended.** Be especially sensitive. For example, do not use the term "gal" to refer to a woman (it has the same connotations as "boy" for an African American male). Address the patient as Mr. or Mrs. or by professional title and last name. Be sure to explain and apoligize if you keep a patient waiting (as you should with *all* patients).

- **Religion is important to many African Americans.** Clergy should be allowed to participate when appropriate. Privacy for prayer is important. Health care practitioners may offer to pray with a patient if all parties are comfortable.

FAMILY/GENDER ISSUES

- **Family structure may be nuclear, extended, or matriarchal.** Close friends or church members may be part of a kin support system and referred to by kin terms. Households headed by women are common; in such cases a grandmother or aunt may be the spokesperson. Otherwise, the father or eldest male may be the spokesperson. Decisions may be made by the patient.

CRADLE TO GRAVE

- **Traditionally, only females attend birth.** Practicing folk medicine in the old South, women may crave red clay dirt (pica) when pregnant. Outside the South, the clay was replaced by Argo starch. In large amounts, it can cause constipation. In small amounts, it may be a comfort.

CRADLE TO GRAVE (CONTINUED)

- **After birth, the mother may delay bathing until post-partum bleeding stops.** Offer a sponge bath. Because menstruation is thought to rid the body of dirty, excess blood, any variation may be feared. If the flow is too light, "bad blood" may back up; if too heavy, the body can weaken. Keep these fears in mind when discussing birth control methods.

- **Those of lower socioeconomic status may be present-time oriented, which may impede preventive medicine and follow-up care. Explain the need for preventive medication (such as for hypertension) or to finish antibiotics even when symptoms disappear.** Explanations may be important. Some may delay seeing a physician until symptoms are severe. Some consider it taboo to donate organs or blood, except to a family member, for fear it will hasten one's own death.

HEALTH-RELATED BELIEFS AND PRACTICES

- **Natural causes of disease include improper diet and exposure to cold/wind; unnatural causes might be God's punishment and voodoo.** Treatment should fit the cause. For example, patients (usually from the South or rural areas) may see gastrointestinal distress as voodoo poisoning, which must be treated by a voodoo practitioner (root doctor).

- **Rich foods (red) may be thought to cause "high" blood, which may be confused with high blood pressure. "High" blood may be treated with clear, white foods to "lower" blood.** Since white foods can include things high in sodium, this should be discussed with the patient. "Low" blood is thought to result from too much vinegar, lemon juice, and garlic, and not enough red meat. Be sure to clarify the difference among "low" blood, low blood count, and low blood pressure.

- **The African American culture has a rich tradition of herbal remedies.** Be sure to discuss the use of home or herbal remedies to prevent potential drug interactions.

NOTE: This material, drawn mainly from the work of Loudell Snow, applies largely to low income uneducated African Americans, especially in the South. See also Walter C.M. and Locks, S. (2005) African Americans. In JG Lipson, SL Dibble, and PA Minarik (Eds.), *Culture and Clinical Care* (pp. 14-26). San Francisco: UCSF Nursing Press.

ANGLO AMERICAN

CAUTION: These are broad generalizations and should not be used to stereotype any individuals.

VALUES, WORLD VIEW, AND COMMUNICATION

- **The individual expects to know the details of his/her condition.** Both direct eye contact and emotional control are expected. But try to avoid excessive direct eye contact with members of the opposite sex to avoid any hint of sexual impropriety.

- **Privacy is important,** yet the patient may want/expect nurses to provide psychosocial care.

FAMILY/GENDER ISSUES

- **Generally, family size is small; the immediate family refers to spouse, siblings, parents, and children.** The individual makes his/her own choices. Because husbands and wives may have equal authority, either parent makes decisions for the child.

CRADLE TO GRAVE

- **Prenatal care is generally sought. The husband is usually the preferred labor partner.** Hospital births are generally preferred, even if an alternative birthing center is used. This may be related to a cultural desire to control events.

- **This culture has no post-partum rituals.** Breast feeding may be practiced for 3 to 6 months.

- **Patients will generally want to know a diagnosis and prognosis.** Independence is highly valued; self-care will generally be accepted. Lower income people tend to be present-oriented; middle- and upper-class individuals tend to be future-oriented.

- **Patients will tend to be stoic, although most will want pain medication.** A patient may prefer to be left alone when sick. Stoicism is valued when someone dies.

- **Organ donations and autopsies are acceptable, as are cremation or burial, unless forbidden by the patient's religion.**

ANGLO AMERICAN

HEALTH-RELATED BELIEFS AND PRACTICES

- **Patients generally prefer an aggressive approach to treating illness.** Biomedicine is preferred, although many may also use complementary and alternative medicine. Be sure to inquire about the use of herbal remedies in a nonjudgmental manner.

- **Germs are thought to cause disease; patients expect treatment to destroy germs.** Antibiotics are often requested, even for viral illnesses.

ASIAN

CAUTION: These are broad generalizations and should not be used to stereotype any individuals. They are most applicable to the least acculturated members.

VALUES, WORLD VIEW, AND COMMUNICATION

- **To show respect, patients may agree to anything you say, without having any intention of following through.** Make sure the reasons for compliance are explained and stressed. Avoid asking questions requiring a "yes" or "no" response. Find a way to have the patient demonstrate an understanding of what you expect.

- **As a sign of respect, patients might avoid direct eye contact.** Do not assign other meanings to this. Avoid hand gestures in case they are offensive; for example, beckoning with the index finger is insulting to Filipinos and Koreans.

- **Offer things several times; patients may refuse at first to be polite.** And realize that because pronouns do not exist in most Asian languages, patients may confuse "he" and "she."

FAMILY/GENDER ISSUES

- **Allow family members to fulfill their familial duty by spending as much time as possible with the patient and by providing non-technical care.** Involve the family in decision-making.

- **Accept that wives may defer to husbands in decision-making and that sons may be valued more than daughters.** And recognize that Asian culture is hierarchical; tremendous respect is often accorded to the elderly.

CRADLE TO GRAVE

- **The patient's "birth partner" may be her mother-in-law or other female relative.**

- **Parents may avoid naming the baby for up to 30 days.** Very traditional new mothers might also avoid cold, bathing, and exercise for one month post-partum ("doing the month"). Respect post-partum prescriptions for rest. Sponge baths and warm liquids may be preferred.

CRADLE TO GRAVE (CONTINUED)

- **Because pregnancy is thought to be a yang or "hot" condition in traditional Chinese medicine, birth is believed to deplete the body of heat.** Restoration of warmth is important. Offer liquids other than ice water, which may be deemed too yin or "cold."

- **Women may be stoic while giving birth.** In fact, Asian patients generally may not express pain. Offer pain medication when the condition warrants it, even if patient does not request it. Insist upon giving it when necessary.

- **When a patient is terminal, family members may wish to shield him/her from that fact.** Ask the patient upon admission (or before the need arises, if possible) whom should be given information about his/her condition.

HEALTH-RELATED BELIEFS AND PRACTICES

- **In China, Korea, and Vietnam, coining and cupping are traditional medical practices, not forms of abuse**. Fevers are often treated by wrapping in warm blankets and drinking warm liquids.

- **Avoid giving ice water, unless requested.** Patients may prefer hot liquids, such as tea. The use of herbs is common. Be sure to instruct recent immigrants on how to use Western medication.

- **Avoid the number 4. Because the character for number 4 is pronounced the same as the character for the word "death," it may signify death for Chinese, Japanese, and Korean patients.** If possible, avoid putting patients in room 4 or operating room 4.

- **Mental illness can be highly stigmatizing in Asian countries.** Patients with emotional problems are likely to present with physical complaints. Patients may be reluctant to discuss emotional problems with strangers, even professionals.

CAUTION: These are broad generalizations and should not be used to stereotype any individuals. They are most applicable to the least acculturated members.

VALUES, WORLD VIEW, AND COMMUNICATION

- **This culture values personal relationships**. Asking about the patient's family and interests before focusing on health issues will generally increase rapport and trust.

FAMILY/GENDER ISSUES

- **Allow family members to express their love and concern by spending as much time as possible with the patient.** Allow them to assist the patient with the activities of daily living if the patient is reluctant to do self-care.

- **Realize that patients may not discuss emotional problems outside the family.** Modesty is important, especially among older women; try to keep them covered whenever possible.

- **Accept that older, more traditional wives may defer to husbands in decision-making, both for their own health and that of their children.** Involve the family in decision-making.

CRADLE TO GRAVE

- **Pregnancy is seen as a normal condition, so prenatal care may not be sought.** In labor and delivery, the woman's mother may be the preferred birthing partner. Laboring women may yell out "aye yie yie"—a loud form of controlled breathing. Others may be stoic.

- **Traditionally, new mothers may avoid cold, bathing, and exercise for six weeks post-partum.** Respect post-partum prescriptions for rest. Sponge baths may be preferred.

- **Pregnancy is considered a "hot" condition; birth is thought to deplete the body of heat.** Restoration of warmth is important. Offer liquids other than ice water, which may be deemed too "cold."

CRADLE TO GRAVE (CONTINUED)

- **While patients may tend to be expressive (loud) when in pain, males may be more expressive around family members than around health care professionals.**

- **The culture tends toward a present-time orientation, which may impede preventive medicine and follow-up care.** Explain the need for preventive medication (such as for hypertension) and to finish antibiotics even after symptoms have disappeared.

- **Family members may want to withhold a fatal diagnosis from the patient; ask the patient upon admission (or before the need arises, if possible) whom should be given information about his/her condition.**

HEALTH-RELATED BELIEFS AND PRACTICES

- **Patients may refuse certain foods or medications that upset a hot/cold body balance.** Offer alternative foods and liquids. Avoid ice water, unless requested.

- **Among traditional women, fat is seen as healthy.** Many Mexican foods are high in fat and salt. Nutritional counseling may be necessary for diabetics and individuals with high blood pressure.

- **Some may believe that complimenting a child without touching him/her can cause evil eye.** To be safe, touch the child when admiring him/her.

- **Ask what herbal remedies, if any, the patient uses.** While most are effective or neutral, azarcón (a bright reddish-orange powder) and greta (a yellow to grayish-yellow powder), used to treat empacho (stomach pain), contain lead and can be dangerous.

CAUTION: These are broad generalizations and should not be used to stereotype any individuals.

Orthodox, Conservative, and Reform designations are based on degree of adherence to, and interpretation of, the Torah and Jewish tradition. Orthodox Jews are most adherent, Reform Jews the least. Israeli Jews may or may not be religious.

VALUES, WORLD VIEW, AND COMMUNICATION

- **Knowledge is highly valued.** Patients may ask a lot of questions. Health is often a source of great concern.

- **Family is often expected to care for the sick.** They are usually interested and involved in the patient's diagnosis, treatment, and personal care.

FAMILY/GENDER ISSUES

- **Sexual segregation is important to the Orthodox.** Married women may cover their heads with a wig or scarf and may not shake hands with men, including health care providers. Orthodox women may prefer a female doctor (although male physicians are allowed). Female nurses should be assigned whenever possible.

CRADLE TO GRAVE

- **A future-time orientation is common.**

- **A husband may not touch his wife when she is bleeding vaginally;** thus, some Orthodox husbands may not attend their wives during labor, or if they do, they may avoid touching them.

- **Males are circumcised on the 8th day after birth,** either at the hospital or at home or the synagogue during a ritual ceremony performed by a specialist (a *mohel*).

- **The body of the deceased is washed and dressed by someone Jewish according to a prescribed ritual.** The Jewish Burial Society may do this task. If hospital staff must touch the body, they should wear gloves. Someone may watch over the body. The body is not embalmed and is buried within 24 hours if possible.

CRADLE TO GRAVE (CONTINUED)

- **Some do not believe in organ donation** because religious laws forbid disfiguring the body; however, others believe it is their duty to donate to save a fellow human being. Some do not believe in harvesting organs from a brain-dead but still breathing patient.

- **Jewish law forbids autopsies unless required by law.** The Orthodox may bury amputated limbs or bloody clothing because the body must be buried whole.

- **There is no set belief about an afterlife.**

HEALTH-RELATED BELIEFS AND PRACTICES

- **Patients may be more concerned with the meaning of pain than with the sensation itself.** For example, Does this mean I have cancer? How can I support my family if I can't work?

- **For Orthodox and Conservative Jews, the Sabbath (sundown Friday to sundown Saturday) is for rest and religious observance.** Orthodox Jews do not touch money, write, or use electrical appliances, including bed controls, call buttons, light switches, elevators, cars, and so on. A non-Jewish person may operate these controls for the patient. Elective surgery should not be performed on the Sabbath, nor should patients be discharged because they cannot travel. Ultra Orthodox patients may refuse to take non-life-saving medications on the Sabbath.

- **The highest Jewish law is that you must do everything you can to save a life,** even if it means violating all the other laws.

- **Observant Jews follow a kosher diet.** They eat only ritually slaughtered meat; they do not eat pork or shellfish or mix meat and dairy.

- **While praying, Orthodox men may wear a shawl and *tfillin* (boxes containing Biblical verses attached to the arm and forehead with leather straps). They may also wear a *yarmulke* (skull cap).**

- Some Orthodox men do not shave, while others do but not with a straight-edge razor.

MIDDLE EASTERN

CAUTION: These are broad generalizations and should not be used to stereotype any individuals. They are most applicable to the least acculturated &/or most religious Muslim members.

VALUES, WORLD VIEW, AND COMMUNICATION

- **Effective communication will often be two-way.** You may need to share information about yourself before these patients will share information about themselves. Health care providers may be expected to take a personal interest in their patients.

- **Try to avoid direct eye contact with members of the opposite sex to avoid any hint of sexual impropriety.**

- **Islam is a dominant force in the lives of many Middle Easterners.** Give patients the privacy to pray several times a day, facing east toward Mecca. Many have a fatalistic attitude regarding health: it's all in Allah's hands, so they may see their health-related behavior as being of little consequence. They may not want to plan for birth or death, since doing so can be seen as challenging the will of Allah.

FAMILY/GENDER ISSUES

- **Be patient with "demanding" family members; they may see it as their job to make sure that the patient gets the best care possible.** It is usually appropriate to speak first to the family spokesman. Repetition of demands is often made to show emphasis, as is a loud tone of voice.

- **Sexual segregation can be extremely important. Assign same-sex caregivers whenever possible, and respect a woman's modesty at all time.** Accept the fact that women may defer to husbands for decision-making about their own and their children's health. In fact, the husband may answer questions addressed to his wife.

- **Personal problems are usually taken care of within the family; they may not be receptive to counseling.**

CRADLE TO GRAVE

- **Patients might not make many preparations for birth.** It is acceptable for women to be very loud and expressive during labor and delivery, after someone has died, and when they are in pain. Male circumcision is common.

- **They may be reluctant to agree to DNR (Do Not Resuscitate) or to plan for death.** Also, they might not allow organ donation or autopsy, because according to Islam, the body should be returned to Allah in the condition in which it was given.

HEALTH-RELATED BELIEFS AND PRACTICES

- **Damp, cold, and drafts may be thought to lead to illness.** Strong emotions are also suspect. For example, the "evil eye" (envy) may be thought to cause illness or misfortune. Amulets to prevent this may be worn and should not be removed. The patient may feel slighted if not given a prescription.

- **When providing meals, be aware that observant Muslims do not eat pork.**

NATIVE AMERICAN

CAUTION: These are broad generalizations and should not be used to stereotype any individuals. They are most applicable to the least acullturated members.

VALUES, WORLD VIEW, AND COMMUNICATION

- **Anecdotes or metaphors may be used by the patient to talk about his/her own situation.** For example, a story about an ill neighbor may be a way of saying the individual is experiencing the same symptoms.

- **Long pauses often indicate that careful consideration is being given to a question.** Do not rush the patient. Loudness is often associated with aggressiveness and should be avoided.

- **Due to history of misuse of signed documents, some may be unwilling to sign informed consent or advanced directives.** And some may display hostility toward health care providers due to history of treatment of Native Americans by whites.

FAMILY/GENDER ISSUES

- **Extended family is important, and any illness concerns the entire family.**

- **Decision-making varies with kinship structure.** Patients will generally make their own decisions.

CRADLE TO GRAVE

- **A female relative may be the birth attendant.** Stoicism is encouraged during labor and delivery. The mother and infant may stay inside and rest for 20 days post-partum or until the umbilical cord falls off, depending upon custom. Some may want to save the umbilical cord, because it may be seen as having spiritual value.

- **Overall, patients may not express pain, other than by mentioning "I don't feel so good" or "Something doesn't feel right."** Offer pain medication when the condition warrants it, even if patient does not appear to be in pain.

- **Patients are generally oriented to activities rather than the clock.** "Indian time" may run very late.

CRADLE TO GRAVE (CONTINUED)

- **Some tribes may prefer to avoid discussion of terminal prognosis or Do Not Resuscitate (DNR), because they believe that negative thoughts hasten death.** Others will use the information to make appropriate preparations.

- **Some tribes may avoid contact with the dying, while others will want to be at the bedside 24 hours a day.** Visitors may display a jovial attitude so as not to demoralize the patient. Mourning is done in private, away from the patient.

- **The names of deceased relatives may be avoided, but the relationship term (e.g., brother, father, sister) may be used.** After death, wailing and shrieking may occur.

- **Some may want to leave a window open for the soul to leave at death; others may orient the patient's body to a cardinal direction before death.**

HEALTH-RELATED BELIEFS AND PRACTICES

- **Before cutting or shaving hair, check to see if the patient or family wants to keep it.** Realize that in some tribes, cutting hair is associated with mourning.

- **A medicine bag may be worn by the patient.** Do not treat it casually or remove it without discussing it with the patient. If it's absolutely necessary to remove it, allow a family member to do so, keep it as close to the patient as possible, and return it as soon as possible.

- **Food that is blessed (in a traditional religion or Christianity) or tobacco (sacred in some native religions) may be thought to be harmless.** Nutritional and anti-smoking counseling should take this into account. Many traditional foods are high in fat.

- **Traditional healers may be combined with use of Western medicine.** Allow traditional healers to perform rituals whenever possible.

NOTE: The material contained in this profile is adapted from Kramer, J. (1996) American Indians. In JG Lipson, SL Dibble, and PA Minarik (Eds.), *Culture and Nursing Care: A Pocket Guide* (pp. 11-22). San Francisco: UCSF Nursing Press.

RUSSIAN

VALUES, WORLD VIEW, AND COMMUNICATION

- **To help allay the anxiety of family members, provide frequent updates on patient treatments and progress**. These patients may expect nurses to be friendly, warm, and caring—that is, to "feel" for them. They may speak loudly and seem abrasive; this was likely necessary in Russia to get attention in the health care system.

- **Make direct eye contact, be firm, and be respectful.** Use hand gestures and facial expressions when English proficiency is minimal. Address patients as Mr. or Mrs. and last name.

FAMILY/GENDER ISSUES

- **The gender of the provider is usually not an issue, but a patient may prefer to have a family member of the same gender present when receiving personal care.**

CRADLE TO GRAVE

- **Exercise and lifting heavy objects are often avoided during pregnancy.** A female relative is often the preferred labor and delivery partner.

- **Russian women tend to have a high pain threshold and stoic attitude.** Encourage appropriate pain management and pre-medicate for dressing changes or daily care that causes discomfort.

- **Patients and their families may frequently offer small gifts of food or chocolate.** Accept them, as it may be perceived as rude to turn them down.

- **Autopsies and organ donations may be refused due to the sacredness of the body.**

- **Because family members may want to withhold a fatal diagnosis from the patient, ask the patient upon admission (or before the need arises, if possible) whom should be given information about his/her condition.**

HEALTH-RELATED BELIEFS AND PRACTICES

- **Many, especially the elderly, believe that illness results from cold.** Therefore, keep a patient covered, close windows, keep the room warm, and avoid iced drinks, especially if he/she has a fever. These patients may prefer sponge baths to showers.

- **They may not like taking a large number of pills.** Space out medication administration so that as few pills as possible are given at one time. And they may prefer non-pharmacologic interventions for nausea, including lemon slices, ginger ale, mineral water, or weak tea with lemon.

- **Be aware that Russians may practice cupping; the resulting marks should not be misinterpreted as abuse or a symptom.**

NOTE: Information for this profile is based on the work of Peter Anderson, R.N. and from Evanikoff, L.J. (1996) Russions. In JG Lipson, SL Dibble, and PA Minarik (Eds.), *Culture and Nursing Care: A Pocket Guide* (pp.239-249). San Francisco: UCSF Nursing Press.

SOUTH ASIAN

CAUTION: These are broad generalizations and should not be used to stereotype any individuals. They are most applicable to the least acculturated members.

Hindus, Sikhs, and Muslims from India, Pakistan, Bangladesh, Sri Lanka, and Nepal

VALUES, WORLD VIEW, AND COMMUNICATION

- **Direct eye contact may be seen as rude or disrespectful, especially among the elderly.**

- **Silence often indicates acceptance or approval.** In some regions, a side-to-side head bob may indicate agreement or uncertainty. An up-and-down nod may indicate disagreement, while acknowledging what the speaker is saying.

- **Male health care providers should not shake hands with a female, unless she offers her hand first.**

- **Some patients may not want to sign consents; they consider health care professionals to be the authorities and may prefer to have them make the decisions.**

FAMILY/GENDER ISSUES

- **Close female family members may remain with the patient; family members may take over activities of daily living (such as feeding, grooming, etc.) for the patient.** Do not insist upon self-care unless medically necessary.

- **The father or eldest son usually has decision-making power, but generally family members are consulted before decisions are made.** Husbands may answer questions addressed to the wife. Due to their modesty, many patients may prefer same-sex caregivers.

CRADLE TO GRAVE

- **Pregnant Hindu women are often encouraged to eat nuts, raisins, coconuts, and fruits to have a healthy, beautiful baby.** Dried ginger powder, celery seeds, nuts, and puffed lotus seeds may be given to the new Hindu mother to cleanse her system and restore her strength.

CRADLE TO GRAVE (CONTINUED)

- **South Asian women may practice a post-partum lying-in period.** While they are expected to feed the baby, everything else is done for them. Traditionally, female relatives take over. If none are around, the patient may expect nurses to do so.

- **Moaning and screaming are acceptable during the birth of the first child.** Otherwise, these patients tend to be stoic. Observant Muslims may not want narcotics for anything other than severe pain.

- **Some patients may prefer to have a fatal diagnosis given to family member.** The family will then decide whether and how much to reveal to the patient. Discuss this "who" of communication well in advance of need, if possible.

HEALTH-RELATED BELIEFS AND PRACTICES

- **Sikhs are enjoined not to cut their hair or shave their beard.** Their hair will usually be worn in a turban. Consider this before cutting or shaving any hair in preparation for surgery.

- **Observant Hindus will generally not eat meat or fish; some may not eat eggs. Observant Muslims will not eat pork. Muslims may not take medications, eat, or drink from sunrise to sunset during Ramadan (usually mid-October to mid-November).**

- **Those who believe in Ayurvedic medicine (Hindus, Sikhs, and some Muslims) see food in terms of a hot/cold classification, based on qualities inherent in the food rather than on the temperature.** "Hot" foods (meat, fish, eggs, yogurt, honey, and nuts) are given for "cold" conditions such as fever or surgery, especially in winter. "Cold" foods (milk, butter, cheese, fruits, and vegetables) are eaten in the summer and for "hot" conditions, including pregnancy.

NOTE: Most of the material contained in this profile is adapted from Rajwani, R., J. (1996) South Asians. In JG Lipson, SL Dibble, and PA Miarik (Eds.), *Culture and Nursing Care: A Pocket Guide* (pp. 264-279). San Francisco: UCSF Nursing Press.

SOUTHEAST ASIAN

CAUTION: These are broad generalizations and should not be used to stereotype any individuals. They are most applicable to the least acculturated members.

VALUES, WORLD VIEW, AND COMMUNICATION
- **Keep in mind that many are refugees who fled to the U.S. to save their lives rather than simply to improve them.**

- **When accompanied by relatives, address the eldest present, especially if male.** Realize that it may be difficult to obtain an accurate health history, because patients were rarely told the name of illnesses or medicines given or procedures performed.

FAMILY/GENDER ISSUES
- **The area from the waist to the knees is extremely private and should never be exposed.** Same sex practitioners and interpreters are best.

- **Their method of calculating age may vary from ours.** For example, a baby may be considered one year old at birth.

CRADLE TO GRAVE
- **They may not give an accurate count of pregnancies because many count only live births.** A baby may not be seen as "human" until several days old—probably to discourage mothers from bonding too closely in an environment with high infant mortality rates.

- **Some Hmong new mothers may want to take home the placenta for burial.**

- **The head is the seat of life and thus very personal, vulnerable, honorable, and untouchable (except by close intimates), so avoid putting IV lines in an infant's scalp unless necessary, and then, only with explanation.**

- **Vietnamese mothers may appear to have difficulty bonding; this is an illusion.** If they pay little attention to their newborns, it is probably out of fear that if they call attention to how attractive they are, spirits may want to steal the child, which could result in its death.

CRADLE TO GRAVE (CONTINUED)

- **Children may wear "spirit-strings" around their wrist.** They should not be cut. Nor should the neck rings that carry the life-souls of babies be cut.

- **Some may believe that at death parents and grandparents become ancestors who should be worshipped and obeyed, and since these ancestors shape the well-being of living descendants, a child (no matter his/her age) may have trouble agreeing to terminate the care of a parent.**

HEALTH-RELATED BELIEFS AND PRACTICES

- **Patients (especially rural non-Christians) may fear surgery because many believe that souls are attached to different parts of the body and can leave, thus causing illness or death.** Some Hmong believe that when people are unconscious, their souls can wander, so anesthesia is dangerous. Some may believe that if the body is cut or disfigured or parts are amputated, it will forever be in a state of imbalance, and the damaged person will become frequently ill and may be physically incomplete in their next incarnation.

- **Some believe that verbal statements in and of themselves can cause the event and for this reason may not want to discuss potential risks and dangers.** A patient may want to consult a shaman.

- **Cupping and coin rubbing are traditional remedies, not forms of abuse.** Ascertain how and why markings were made before reporting them.

- **Some may have concerns about blood being taken.** They may fear it will sap their strength, cause illness or their soul to leave their body, or it will not be replenished. If a patient is anxious, ask about his or her concerns so they can be addressed.

NOTE: Most of the information for this profile was adapted from Muecke, M.A. (1983) Caring for Southeast Asian Refugee Patients in the USA. *American Journal of Public Health* 73(4): 431-438. Information on Hmong beliefs was taken from Fadiman, A. (1997) *The Spirit Catches You and You Fall Down*. New York: Farrar, Straus and Giroux and Johnson, S. (1996) Hmong. In JG Lipson, SL Dibble, and PA Minarik (Eds.), *Culture and Nursing Care: A Pocket Guide* (pp. 155-168). San Francisco: UCSF Nursing Press.